# SCOUT ISLAND!

## THE STORY OF THE WORLD'S FIRST BOY SCOUT CAMP, AND MORE....

This book is sold subject to the condition that it shall not, by way of trade or otherwise, be lent, re-sold, hired out, photocopied or held in any retrieval system or otherwise circulated without the publisher's prior consent in any form of binding or cover other than that in which this is published and without a similar condition including this condition being imposed on the subsequent purchaser.

Scout Island! ISBN 978-0-9513168-5-6
© copyright Steven Harris, May 2007

Published by Lewarne Publishing
PO Box 26946
London SE21 8XG

www.lewarnepublishing.co.uk

Typesetting and front/back cover designs by MKG, Bridgwater, Somerset
Printed by Kampress, Bridgwater, Somerset

"Look wide, and even when you think you are looking wide - look wider still!"

*Baden-Powell*

"Help to create a better world and a brighter future for the youth of tomorrow."

*Olave Baden-Powell*

# CONTENTS

Introduction ............................................. 7

B.-P.'s Experimental Camp ................... 11

The Camp Kit List ................................. 15

The Four Boy Scout Patrols ................. 16

A Novel Idea ......................................... 17

The Eight Days' Programme ................ 20

Real Memories from the Participants ... 22

B.-P. Describes his Methods ................ 25

The Last Day of the Camp, as
Described by William Hillcourt ............ 26

B.-P.'s Post-Camp Letter ...................... 27

Camp Accounts ..................................... 28

The Commemorative Stone
and its Sculptor .................................... 30

# CONTENTS SECTION TWO

The Handbook *Scouting for Boys* .........32

The Movement Takes Off! .....................35

What about the Girls? ...........................38

The Passing of Scouting's Founder ......40

Famous Former Scouts .........................42

The Scout Movement :
Did You Know? .....................................43

Brownsea Island: Did
You Know? ...........................................46

The Scout Law and Promise .................54

Some Key Scouting Events ...................54

Bibliography
and Acknowledgements ........................56

Baden-Powell, Scouting's Founder

Olave Baden-Powell, World Chief Guide

Text by Steven Harris

# INTRODUCTION

Most people today know the name Baden-Powell. Born 150 years ago, his legacy is a world-wide youth movement for boys and girls of practically all ages, religions, classes and cultures. But to children and adults living in the reign of Queen Victoria, B.-P. (as he came to be affectionately known) was not the founder of a youth movement but a famous soldier. There were cadets and various boys' brigades but no such thing as a Boy Scout movement.

In the days before film and television idols, colonels and generals such as B.-P. were often national and international heroes. After defending the besieged town of Mafeking against the Boer fighters during the South African war, B.-P. became a national hero. His many ruses to keep the enemy at bay, his charismatic manner, and his skills in keeping up morale for 217 days, were read about widely in the '**B**ritish **P**ress' back home.

With the relief of Mafeking on the 17th May 1900, B.-P. instantly became every boy's hero. But he had already been honing his scouting skills in his earlier military career, and a book for army men called *Aids to Scouting* had been published in 1899. With B.-P.'s name featuring in many articles, and his image appearing in portraits, on busts and even on mugs and biscuit tins, B.-P. - as famous as any world-class footballer today - attracted many youths who wanted to try out his scouting ideas even though his army book had been intended for soldiers. Fortunately, after a few years his army book was rewritten and published in a simplified form in boys' papers, including the Boys' Brigade's Gazette in 1906 (B.-P. was a Vice-President of the Boys' Brigade). However, before it was eventually published as a book, an important event took place that would change thousands of boys' lives forever!

Rewriting his army book for boys had been no easy matter. Theory was all very well, what B.-P. really wanted to do was try out his Boy Scouting scheme with real 'guinea pigs'. Luckily, he eventually met a man with influence and finance who could help him. His name was

MAN OF THE HOUR—*The Defender of Mafeking.*

B.-P. ~ He would spend 34 years in the army,
and 34 years in the Scout movement

8					Text by Steven Harris

Arthur Pearson, a wealthy publisher and owner of numerous publications, including the *Evening Standard*.

After writing most of the drafts for *Scouting for Boys* while staying in a house next to the windmill on Wimbledon Common, during that same month of July 1907 B.-P. began to prepare for his forthcoming experimental camp. This had been with the full encouragement and support of Arthur Pearson.

Sir Arthur Pearson

# BROWNSEA ISLAND

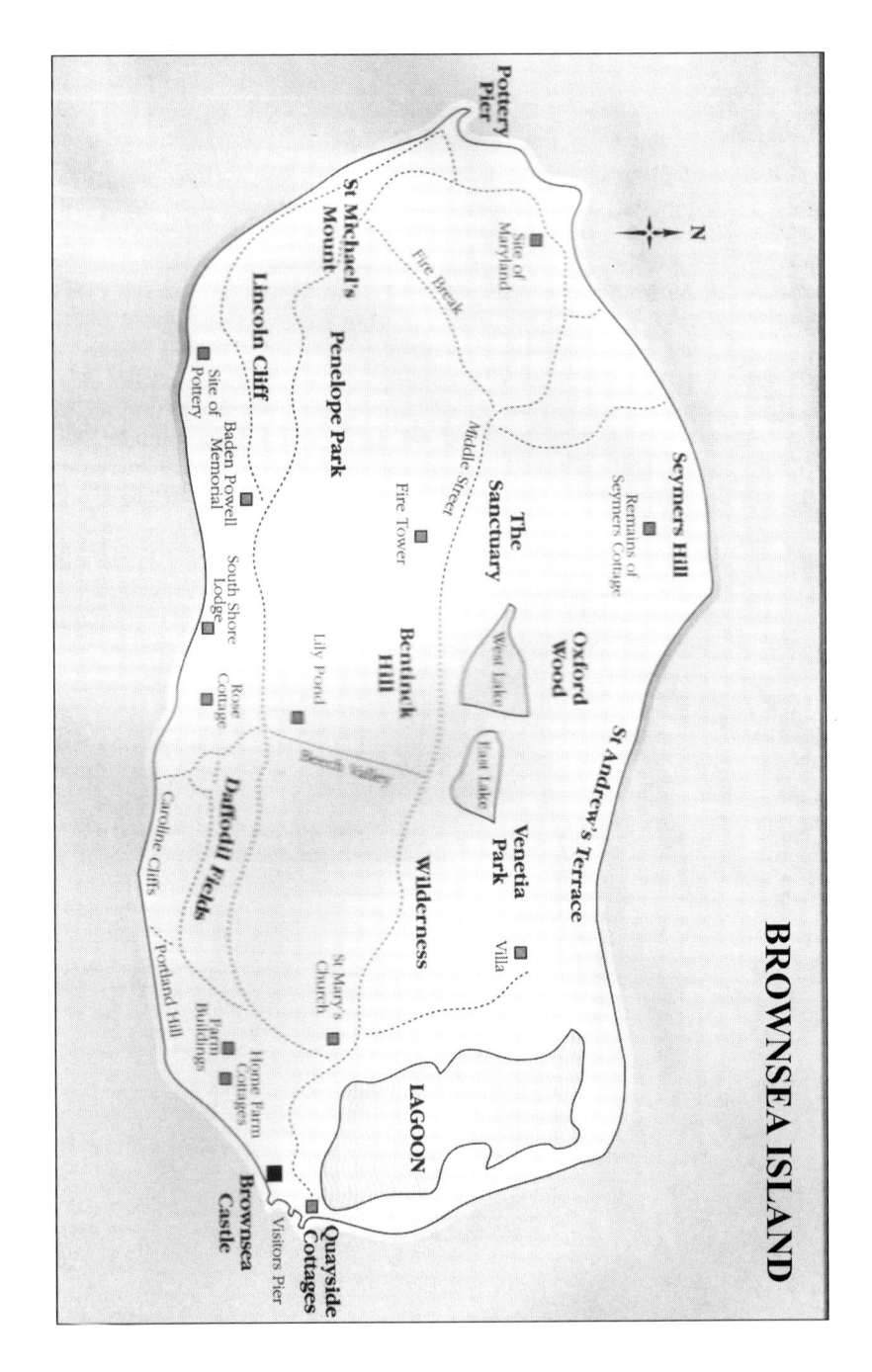

Text by Steven Harris

# B.-P.'S EXPERIMENTAL CAMP

Where to hold the camp? Even though it had been some seven years since B.-P. had risen to fame after his exploits during the siege of Mafeking, he was still very much a household name - he was a frequent guest speaker for organisations such as the YMCA, and could even be seen at Madame Tussauds. He wanted to try out his ideas uninhibited by the press and photographers. Fortunately he'd met Charles van Raalte, a wealthy and affable owner of an island in Dorset, while on holiday fishing in Ireland. Charles and his wife Florence van Raalte were pleased to allow the famous soldier to try out his peculiar boys' scheme on their island (glimpses of it might provide some entertainment for their guests, some of whom were from European royal families).

How fitting that the place Brownsea, near Poole, should incorporate B.-P.'s initials. Such coincidences would abound in later life (notably his wife sharing his birthday, and his son's wife also sharing his wife's birthday). For it turned out that B.-P. was no stranger to Brownsea Island, he and his brothers had once sailed across from Poole Harbour to one of its beaches (even his future wife Olave had sailed around it as a child).

Whilst there was a castle, church and other buildings on the island, B.-P. knew that the 500 or so acres included plenty of secluded spots, and two lakes, where he could run a camp and train the boys in scouting.

Charles van Raalte

Engraving of Brownsea

Once all the boys had arrived, the camp started officially on the 1st August. The 20 boys had been put into four patrols, which were named after animals and birds: the boys were asked to learn the call signs for their particular patrol. They were a deliberate mix of boys from local Boys' Brigade Companies and public school boys from further afield. B.-P. had invited the wealthier boys through knowing them personally or knowing their parents.

The idea of working as a unit - a patrol - with one boy in charge, was very novel, as was the idea of mixing classes. But the whole thing proved to be a great success. The boys were put on their honour to behave well, care for each other and not let the patrol down, and they didn't. The older boys were trained, and they then passed on their knowledge and skills to the younger boys. All the ideas of being on your honour, working and living as a patrol, would become unique components of the Scout system of youth training.

25/7/07, The *Poole Daily Herald* announces the camp:

*BOYS' ENCAMPMENT- Major-Gen. Baden-Powell, whose interest in boys is well known, is arranging for a boys' encampment, which, by the kind permission of Mr. Charles van Raalte, is to be pitched on Brownsea Island next week. This gallant officer has picked out about a score of youths from two or three of the large Public Schools, and there will probably be half a dozen more selected from the local companies of Boys' Brigades. They will go into camp next Monday or Tuesday, and remain under canvas about a week.*

B.-P. and part of the party going over to Brownsea

# The 1907 Brownsea Camp

Text by Steven Harris

# BROWNSEA CAMP KIT LIST

Today Scouts are still given a kit list by their Scout leaders when going to camp. The items suggested in 1907 have not changed that much though asthma inhalers, sun cream, iPods and mobile phones (items sometimes used today) are in striking contrast to 1907!

## CAMP KIT

knife, fork and spoon
2 enamelled plates, 1 mug
waterproof sheet
2 blankets (no sheets)
1 pillow and pillow case
2 rough towels
1 smooth towel
tin cooking billy*
canvas haversack*
2 coat straps 8 inch. long*
jack knife and lanyard*
soap and sponge
toothbrush
brush and comb
small looking glass

## PERSONAL KIT

1 pair of flannel trousers
1 pair of flannel 'shorts'
   or knickerbockers
2 pairs of stockings and garters
   (if possible: green tabs showing
   below the roll of stockings)
2 flannel shirts
neckerchief (preferably dark green)
1 suit pyjamas
1 pair of bathing drawers
sweater or old jacket
cap
hat; preferably grey wideawake,
   for sun
2 pairs of strong boots or shoes
1 pair of slippers or canvas shoes
warm great coat
warm gloves
leather waistbelt
waterproof coat or cape (opt.)
wrist watch (opt.)
compass (opt.)
housewife (sewing kit)

Items marked * were optional but could be bought in camp.

# THE FOUR BOY SCOUT PATROLS

## BULLS
Patrol Leader
Herbert Emley
Ethelbert Tarrant
William Rodney
Herbert Collingbourne
Humphrey Noble

## CURLEWS
Patrol Leader
Bob Wroughton
Cedric Curteis
John Evans-Lombe
Percy Medway
Reginald Giles

## RAVENS
Patrol Leader
Thomas Evans-Lombe
Arthur Primmer
Albert Blandford
James Rodney
Marc Noble

## WOLVES
Patrol Leader
George Rodney
Herbert Watts
J. Alan Vivian
Terence Bonfield
Richard Grant

## Adults and Assistants
Baden-Powell, Camp Leader
Kenneth McLaren, friend and Mafeking veteran
George Green, Quartermaster (and a B. B. Captain)
Henry Robson, Quartermaster (also a B.B. Captain)
William Stevens, Instructor (Coastguard Officer)
Donald Baden-Powell, Adjutant/Orderly to B.-P.
Unnamed Camp Chef (ex-army?)

Notes: Composition of patrols is as per the latest evidence. Not listed by B.-P., it is believed that a sixth boy was in the Curlews Patrol: Charles Rodney (note the numerous brothers). Also, Percy Everett, publisher Arthur Pearson's right-hand man, visited the Camp for several days (he became a key figure in the movement).

# A NOVEL IDEA...

Camping in 1907 was a very novel idea, it was something that almost only the military and gipsies did. Being out under canvas, many parents believed, was likely to lead to their children getting colds, rheumatism, food poisoning or pestered by vagabonds. Hence B.-P.'s reassurances in his letter, which told the Brownsea boys' parents *'wholesome food, cooking and sanitation'* would be used.

The wearing of shorts, too, was quirky. Once again, the boys might suffer from the cold and damp; yet short trousers in camp proved to be comfortable and practical. It didn't take long for fashion to emulate the Boy Scouts, and for many boys and schools to follow suit (admittedly quite often with less baggy alternatives!).

It is interesting that the adults involved with the camp, which involved two Boys' Brigade Captains - George Green and Henry Robson - were 'old' for leaders of a youths' camp. Most were in their late forties or older (B.-P. had turned fifty).

Despite the title of this book, there is no Scout Island really, yet there is a BP Island next to Brownsea - Furzey Island is occupied by BP Plc, and used for oil drilling and research. Brownsea itself was given the name by the van Raaltes, who owned it when B.-P. was running his camp. Charles van Raalte, a prolific entertainer, decided to change the name from Branksea to Brownsea after his guests frequently alighted at Branksome railway station by mistake. This was near to Bournemouth but not Poole.

At the Brownsea Island camp, B.-P. woke the boys each morning with a few blasts on his African Koodoo horn. From a cavalry lance stuck into the ground outside his tent flew the Union flag that had flown outside B.-P.'s headquarters at Mafeking. Before breakfast-proper at 8.00am, the boys would wash, they were then given cocoa to drink and a biscuit. This would tide them over whilst they embarked on half an hour's physical exercises.

Later in the week they were taught how to make their own biscuits. Mums might have been unimpressed that B.-P. instructed the boys to mix the dough recipe in the pockets of their coats. The mixture was then wrapped around sticks and heated on the embers of the fire. With the sand-flies and mosquitoes being nightly visitors, one of the boys, Terry Bonfield, didn't relish the thought of consuming his insect-laden 'dampers' and 'twists'.

A compulsory hour's rest after lunch was the order of the day (no talking!), something many Scout Troops continued to do for decades after.

Initially, B.-P., on occasions, and other Scout authors liked to describe the mix of the social classes as 'Public School boys with boys from the East End of London'. About half the boys were from public schools (including Eton and B.-P.'s former school, Charterhouse), and the other half were from local (Bournemouth and Poole) Boys' Brigade Companies.

Historian Tim Jeal felt the boys in general mixed well, though highlights two opposing observations by the boys themselves:

*...although occasionally each group surprised the other: the public school boys struck the Brigade boys as prissily over-polite, while the Brigade boys sometimes surprised the others by feats such as eating raw cockles. Not yet weaned to oysters, the future Lord Rodney felt sick to watch them.*

Among the many games and activities they were encouraged to try, one was a nightly 'piquet' where one patrol was given rations of flour, potatoes, meat and tea. They were allowed to camp apart from the others, but could be stalked by B.-P. and the others until 11.00pm. But even the camp leader could be caught out when stalking! Donald, B.-P.'s young nephew (and orderly/adjutant), was well placed hiding up in a tree one night. Through failing to look upwards, B.-P. was captured by Donald, who nearly fell on him in his excitement at catching the Defender of Mafeking.

Another game was the Whale Hunt. This entailed two patrols going out in boats and seeing if they could harpoon the whale (not that fast moving as it was made of wood!). There was some decorum, however, as the boys said prayers every day and were expected to dress each evening for dinner, which was eaten in the dining marquee.

# THE EIGHT DAYS' PROGRAMME

Day One
Preliminaries. Duties/orders given. The appointed Patrol Leaders were given their first training.

Day Two
Campaigning: making yourself comfortable in camp. Hut and mat-making, knotting, fire-lighting, cooking, navigation, boat management.

Day Three
Observation, tracking (and using tracking irons), eye-sight and memory training.

Day Four
Woodcraft, nature and animal study, the stars. Also study of people, their habits, gait, characteristics (today called body language).

Day Five
Chivalry and Honour, using the Knights of the Round Table and similar examples. Also helping others and doing a daily good-turn.

Day Six
Saving Life, First-aid, for example: from drowning, sewer gas, runaway horses, fires.

Day Seven
Patriotism. Study of how empires rose and fell; the British Empire, geography, the army and navy, citizenship, country first, self second....

Day Eight
Games/sports that encourage fitness and teamwork. A special farewell display for invited guests.

Final day, Day Nine ~ Time to strike camp and leave!

Text by Steven Harris

Note the patrol colours (tassels) on the boys' left shoulders, and the Scout badge on the right arm (earned after passing some tests)

B.-P. supervising a tug-of-war

1907 – 2007

# REAL MEMORIES FROM THE PARTICIPANTS

### Terry Bonfield, Wolves Patrol
*We were taken by open lorry to Poole - all with our little kit bags. From Sandbanks we went across to the island and walked from the quay to the isolated camp. It was very exciting to a young boy - all very wonderful. We were given a groundsheet and two blankets and were told to use the kit-bag as a pillow. We scooped out a little hole for our hips. I slept like a log.*

### Humphrey Noble, Bulls Patrol
*In the evening we gathered round the camp fire. There was no Summer Time then or Daylight Saving in those days so that it was dark at a reasonable hour; and B.-P. would tell us stories. He was a wonderful teller of tales and had had the most exciting adventures and escapes during his Army life, culminating naturally in the famous Defence of Mafeking. He had a very clear resonant voice which arrested attention from the very first. So you can imagine us sitting there in the darkness round the fire listening spell-bound to some thrilling story.*

### Arthur Broomfield
A local lad, not in any patrol, he even does a good-turn for B.-P.! ~
*By 1907 most of my brothers and sisters had grown up and left the island. I was the only one still at school. It was during the long summer holiday that Baden-Powell arrived, and so I had plenty of spare time in which to follow closely all that happened. My father told me to keep away from the camp unless I was invited to go there, so for a while I had to be content to look on from a distance. Every day I went to a vantage point a few hundred yards from the camp and watched the busy preparations ...*

*Sometimes I would row slowly along close inshore to get a better view. This eventually led to my being hailed by some of the boys, and*

*I invited them to come out for a pull in the dinghy. Gradually I made friends with them, and I began to take part in their Scouting activities. Tracking and woodcraft were already second nature to me, and I knew every plant, animal and bird on my island home.*

*Then came the memorable meeting with Baden-Powell himself. The founder of the Scouts had been my hero for many years. I never tired of reading about his many exploits in Africa and other lands. The siege and relief of Mafeking was one of my earliest memories of outstanding events in the Boer War. I remember, too, the Baden-Powell mug which I carried home so proudly. You can imagine the thrill I felt when I met my hero face to face.*

Eye and memory training

*One evening in August I was walking along the path that led from my home to the camp. It was very hot. Nightjars were burring away in the trees, and the mosquitoes were humming around in clouds as I scuffed my way along a path carpeted with slippery pine needles. Bracken grew waist-high on either side. On my right rose the pine-clad hillside, and on my left the heather and gorse-covered ground sloped down to the sea.*

*I had reached the point where the camp came into sight when I heard someone calling me. I looked down the hill and saw a man floundering in a patch of bog. There were many such patches near the camp, where one might sink knee-deep in soft rust-coloured mud.*

*I ran across the rough ground and showed the stranger the way out of the bog. As he came towards me I realised that he was none other than Baden-Powell himself. I was too overwhelmed to speak audibly as he clasped my hand, and asked my name and where I lived. I grabbed a handful of bracken, and wiped the mud from his shoes and stockings. The great man smiled down at me, patted my shoulder and thanked me for helping him. Then, proud and excited, I ran home to tell my parents about my adventure.*

*After that I saw Baden-Powell again several times, when I was invited to join the Scouts round their camp fire, and I listened with rapt attention to his stories.*

Text by Steven Harris

# B.-P. LATER DESCRIBES HIS METHODS IN *CHUMS* BOYS' COMIC

B.-P. seemed to have an instinctive feel for how boys learnt best, his ideas were well ahead of teaching methods in schools. He believed in not lecturing, or at least keeping talk to the minimum, and allowing boys plenty of practical activities. Tracking, for example, was practised with special tracking irons and using sandy areas of the island. In his piece in *Chums* B.-P. illustrates how tracking and observation were made into fun activities:

*At the camp fire over night we would tell the boys some interesting instances of the value of being able to track. Next morning we would teach them reading tracks by making footmarks of different paces, and showing how to read them and deduce their meaning. In the afternoon we would have a game such as 'Deer-Stalking,' in which one boy went off as the deer armed with half a dozen tennis balls. Twenty minutes later four hunters went off after him, following his tracks, each hunter armed with a tennis ball. The deer after going a mile or two would hide and endeavour to ambush his hunters, and so to get them within range; each hunter hit with his tennis ball was counted gored to death. If, on the other hand, he was hit three times by their balls he was killed.*

# THE LAST DAY OF THE CAMP
## (AS DESCRIBED BY AUTHOR WILLIAM HILLCOURT)

*B.-P. had intended it to be the 'proof-of-the- pudding' occasion and had invited the parents of the boys, the van Raaltes and their guests, and all the islanders to come to Battery Hill to witness the boys putting on a display of their skills they had learned. Percy W. Everett, editorial manager for C. Arthur Pearson Ltd., came down from London on behalf of his firm to find out how well Baden-Powell's experimental camp had succeeded.*

*The show became an extraordinary performance - completely boy-planned, boy-led and boy executed. It was a mixture of games and competitions, of demonstrations of first aid and firemanship, of mat weaving and ju-jitsu. It ended in a tug-of-war between the 'birds' (the Curlews and the Ravens) and the 'beasts' (the Wolves and the Bulls), won by the 'birds'. Time and again the audience broke into appreciative applause. And when the show was over, the van Raaltes invited the whole camp to Brownsea Castle for a banquet-like tea in the beautiful dining-room, with a brass band from Poole playing on the terrace outside. At the call of one of their number, the boys gave three cheers for the 'best General in the world' and three more for their hosts, then returned to their tents and to the sad task of beginning to strike camp.*

*Baden-Powell:*
*The Two Lives of a Hero,*
*1964*

Text by Steven Harris

# B.-P.'S POST-CAMP LETTER TO ONE OF THE FATHERS

### (Reproduced in *The Scouter* July 1957)

B.-P. was always a good letter writer. Whenever he was asked to inspect boys at a rally or similar function he would write a letter of thanks a few days after. The letter would always be polite but invariably carried constructive comments on what had gone well and what could be improved upon next time. Writing to the father of Marc and Humphrey Noble, two brothers who had participated in the experimental camp on Brownsea, B.-P. wrote a day after the camp:

*Thank you so much, my dear Noble, for your very kind letter. It was a very great pleasure to have two such nice little fellows as your boys in my camp. I hope they got home all safely and none the worse for their outing.*

*This camp was to a large extent experimental - merely to try in practice the details of my bigger scheme before issuing them in book form. And I am delighted to find they worked out so well as they did.*

*But before I can be sure of their success I want to hear from the parents themselves what they think of it. They are the best judges...*

# CAMP ACCOUNTS

The Camp made a loss! B.-P. had apparently not troubled himself too much about budgeting or covering costs. No doubt he wouldn't have wanted to deter the local boys from attending through lack of funds; on the other hand, he wouldn't have wanted to patronise any of the twenty boys by not allowing them to contribute towards their board and 'lodgings' (the letter below confirms that B.-P. was quite prepared to invest some of his own money in the experiment). Still, the launch of a new youth movement for about £55.00 was a bargain!

| Expended | 13 boys messing | @ £1.00 | £ 13. 00.0 |
| --- | --- | --- | --- |
| | 9 town boys | @ 3/6 | £ 1. 11.6 |
| | donations | | £ 16. 00.0 |
| | | | £ 30.11.6 |
| | Total amount expended | | £ 55.02.8 |
| | Leaving a deficit of | | £ 24.11.2 |

Fortunately Saxon Noble, the father of the two Noble boys, volunteered to help settle the deficit. B.-P. wrote to him:

*It was awfully kind of you to offer to help me in the matter of expenses - I am afraid that they may come a bit higher than I had at first estimated - but I always intended to spend something myself as a necessary step towards getting the scheme perfected. So as the camp was in this way partly for the benefit of the scheme I thought it right that the boy whom I was using in this experiment should merely defray some of the cost - i.e. the bare expenses of their food etc.*

*But unexpected expenses have cropped up ....So that a little help would probably be very acceptable indeed.*

B.-P., reflecting on the Camp afterwards, wrote:

*Since this experimental camp I am more than ever convinced of the possibilities that underlie the Scouts training as an educator of boys of all classes.*

*Prepared as I was for enthusiastic endeavour on the part of the lads, I was surprised at the effect on their character which became visible even in the few days we were at work. And I have not trusted merely to my own observation, but have had reports from the parents bearing out this conclusion, and giving incidentally some very useful hints from the parents' point of view.*

The above reveals something of B.-P.'s wonderful belief in boys, he had a unique ability in seeing their potential, knowing they needed nurturing. His humour, too, often appealed to boys, as seen in many of his sketches.

**TOMMY THE TENDERFOOT SERIES.**

No 4.

FIRE LIGHTING.
On lighting of fires he set everyone right.
But his own little bonfire refused to ignite.

# THE COMMEMORATIVE STONE AND ITS SCULPTOR

Don Potter, a man with an apposite name, was responsible for sculpting the commemorative stone that has sat on its plinth near the site of the original camp since 1967. The 2.5 metres piece of Portland stone was unveiled by the Baden-Powells' daughter, the Hon. Mrs Betty Clay. In fact Don Potter usually had a hand in selecting the quarry and actual stone for his work. A great artist and friend of B.-P.'s, also a former Wolf Cub, Scout and employee/carver at Gilwell Park, Don Potter sculpted a 15 cwt portrait bust for the Scouts of the Dominican Republic in 1958 (also the small bust that can be seen on the wall of Brownsea Island castle garden). Additionally, his well known statue of B.-P. still stands outside Baden-Powell House in South Kensington, London. (Present at the unveiling, he was gently ticked off for not wearing Scout uniform!)

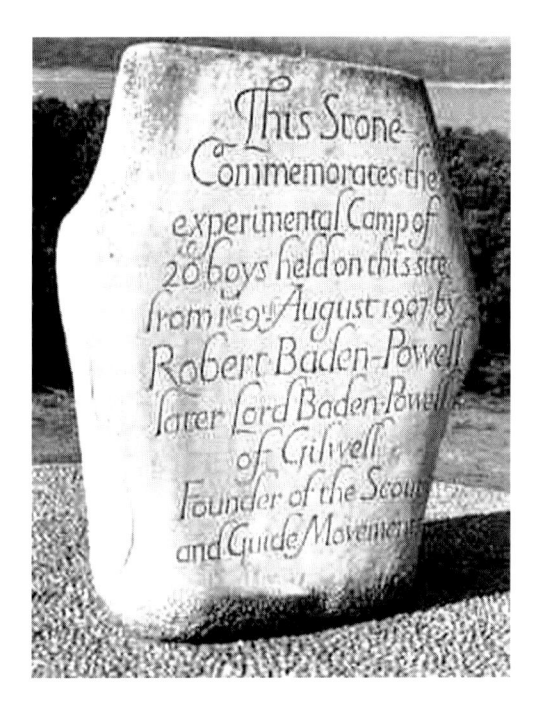

Text by Steven Harris

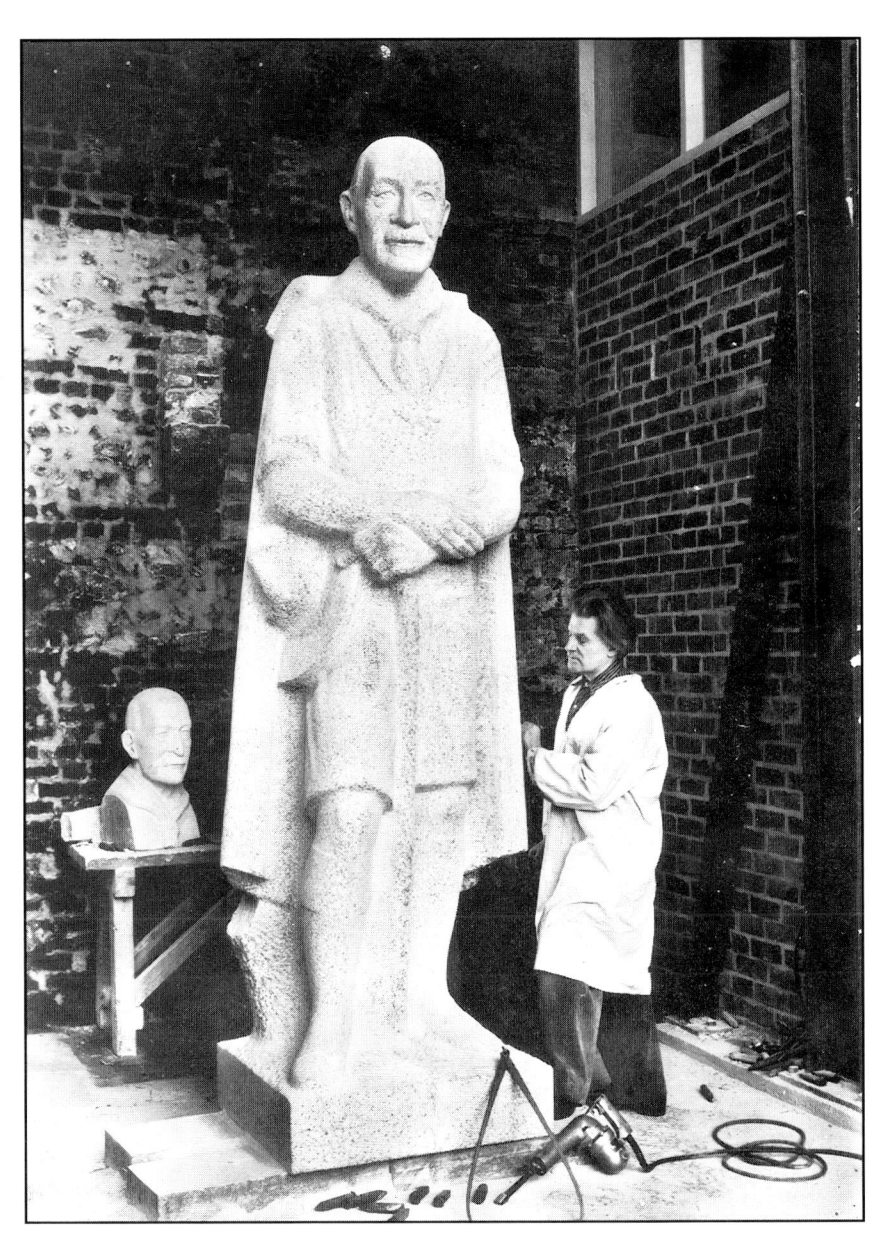

Don Potter putting the finishing touches

1907 – 2007

# SECTION TWO
# THE HANDBOOK *SCOUTING FOR BOYS*

B.-P. wrote a report of the camp in the autumn, and began a series of lectures to youth leaders and boys around the country. His handbook *Scouting for Boys* was initially published in fortnightly parts starting 15th January 1908 (priced 4d). Although it was a serial that many boys (adults too) began to collect and read with awe and excitement, initially it did not receive great reviews in the local and national press. Despite the many inspiring anecdotes and sketches from B.-P.'s own hand, its layout and content might have appeared quirky to some adults. It had been a somewhat rushed affair and was produced on cheap paper (to help make it affordable to most boys). Although generally respectful and optimistic, some reviewers couldn't see how working-class boys from the towns and cities were going to be attracted to what they perceived to be B.-P.'s 'a life on the prairie' approach. Wearing shorts, walking around with broomsticks, doing things for others? It'll never take off!

The first complete handbook came out on 1st May in the same year it was first published, and was reprinted four times in its first year of publication (though no precise sales figures have survived).

B.-P. ploughed all profits from the book into organising and developing his Boy Scouts scheme (which initially included paying the salaries of the small nucleus of Headquarters staff working from a tiny London office).

By 1909 it had been translated into five languages. Jeal also notes:

*Twenty years after its first publication in Great Britain, the book was in print in 26 countries (not including all those within the British Empire) in roughly twice that many editions.... 'Scouting for Boys' has probably sold more copies than any other title during the twentieth century with the exception of the Bible.*

Both Welsh and Braille editions have also been published.

More than 50,000 copies were sold in Britain forty years later, in 1948, the fortieth anniversary of its first publication.

The book was revised frequently and a thinner boys' edition was published also. In 1963 a 'definitive' edition was published which included many sketches by B.-P. previously unseen in the book.

The front covers for the original parts of S for B published on 15th January 1908 were designed by John Hassall. Born in Walmer, Kent, he became a well known illustrator. A member of the London Sketch Club (as was B.-P.), he pioneered modern poster design. 'Skegness is so bracing', one of his railway posters, holds the record for longevity and ubiquity (though he had never been to Skegness at the time of designing the poster!).

April 1999 saw the 5th printing of the 35th edition of S for B. It was last published in 2004 (by OUP). Although it has not been officially used as a handbook for several decades, sales continue in a steady stream, year by year.

The complete handbook was published on the 1st May 1908, priced 2/- cloth covered or 1/- in paper.

Text by Steven Harris

# THE MOVEMENT TAKES OFF !

Beginnings at Brownsea, then boys buy boots, big hats, broomsticks and follow Baden-Powell... Actually, many boys made their own uniforms by cutting long trousers down and dyeing shirts or jumpers. Ex-Boer War hats could be purchased from the Army and Navy stores. The original uniform was deliberately minimal and 'non-showy' so as not to deter poorer boys from joining.

## Brownsea stands for...

- **B** ~ B is for Boy Scout and big hat: a Stetson or 'lemon squeezer' was the Scout's unofficial trademark (even though B.-P. opted to wear a trilby at the Brownsea camp); the Boy Scout also wore a leather bottle-opener belt.
- **R** ~ rope: every good Boy Scout carried a hank of rope on his belt. He might need to rescue a runaway horse, pull someone from the ice, or....
- **O** ~ overcoat: carried just in case... It made a good groundsheet too. O is also for the Oath (Promise), something every good Scout lived by.
- **W** ~ whistle, blown to raise the alarm; and water bottles: very important before convenience drinks and plentiful corner shops.
- **N** ~ neckerchief: many Scouts called their scarves by this informal term. Great for bandages and other uses. More equipment was carried in the napsack/haversack.
- **S** ~ socks, shirt and shorts (called knickers in those days!). Scout sleeves were supposed to be rolled up (on the inside) so as to be ever ready; socks had garter tabs as spare darning material.
- **E** ~ emergency tin with matches, coins, plasters etc.; epaulettes: shirt straps for (later) holding the beret.
- **A** ~ axe. Yes, the original Boy Scout never felt complete without his axe. With his kit complete, the Scout was ready for action, to boldly go where no Scout had ever gone before!

Whether it was Scotland or Cornwall, from 1908 Boy Scout Patrols and Troops sprang up all over Britain. The photo above depicts Scouts of the 1st Par Troop in Cornwall. They, like the 1st Glasgow Scout Troop, were founded in 1908, and both are still thriving today.

Text by Steven Harris

Scouting was an incredibly flexible idea. Branches were designed to cater for younger and older boys - Wolf Cubs and Rover Scouts - and also for those interested in sea and air activities.

Actor Laurence Olivier, then an RAF Lieutenant, speaking to Air Scouts at the first All England Air Scout Camp, 1942

# WHAT ABOUT THE GIRLS?

Some girls were envious of their brothers having all the fun, others of them saw boys going on treks and camps: it seemed much more fun than staying at home reading, knitting, or looking after baby Johnny!

It just wasn't the done thing for older boys and girls to mix together. In many schools there were separate entrances for boys and girls; P.E. lessons, too, were often not done together. B.-P., a very busy man (still employed by the army until 1910), knew his Scout scheme could be applied to all sorts of organisations, including those for girls. It took time but eventually he drew up a girls' scheme with the help of his sister, Agnes. It was agreed to call this sister organisation the Girl Guides, and they were officially started in 1910. Until a special handbook was written for the new organisation, they too used *Scouting for Boys*.

The B.-P. family

Text by Steven Harris

Left:

The Brownsea Acorn

Below:

The first three figures (left to right) are surviving members of the first-ever Scout Camp.

Taken on Brownsea in 1965, they are Arthur Primmer, Terry Bonfield and Reg Giles.

1907 – 2007

# THE PASSING OF SCOUTING'S FOUNDER

By the time of the Second World War, B.-P. and Olave had settled in Nyeri, South Africa. He had become increasingly unwell. Sadly, on the 8th January 1941 he passed away. Born in the Victorian era, he had witnessed enormous changes in his 83 years. He was buried in St. Peter's Church, Nyeri. Many memorial services were held in churches around Britain; a national memorial service for the life of Baden-Powell was held in Westminster Abbey on the 27th January.

B.-P.'s funeral cortege

Text by Steven Harris

# The Scout

**6d**

1907 – 2007

# FAMOUS FORMER SCOUTS

There are hundreds of well known people who have been members of the Scout movement. And also the Girl Guide movement: H M The Queen, Betty Boothroyd, Cherie Blair, Angela Ripon, Claire Short MP, Joan Plowright, Glenda Jackson CBE, Anneka Rice, Jayne Torvill...

England footballer David Beckham is a former Scout. In his autobiography David Beckham wrote: *I was a Cub and later went on to be a Scout, both of which involved football, so I was happy doing that. Also, we'd go camping and it was great to go away with a group of friends. You learn quite a bit about yourself when you're away from your family.*

**Sport**
Graham Hill, Sir Stirling Moss, Brian and Nigel Clough, Sir Trevor Brooking, Michael Owen...

**Music**
Sir Cliff Richard, Sir Paul McCartney, Val Doonican, David Grant, George Michael...

**Comedy**
Ken Dodd, Ronnie Corbett, Les Dawson, Jim Davidson, Harry Hill, Matt Lucas...

**Acting**
Sir John Mills, Sir Norman Wisdom, Lord Richard Attenborough, Derek Jacobi, Edward Woodward, Martin Shaw...

**Others**
Sir Richard Branson, Prince Andrew, Simon Mayo, Chris Tarrant, Russell Grant, David Bellamy, Michael Buerk, Sir Michael Parkinson, David Bannatyne.

# THE SCOUT MOVEMENT: DID YOU KNOW?

In the 1970s it was said that one in four men in the UK had at some point been in the Scouts.

Leaders in the movement are all volunteers and undergo a strict vetting procedure.

All Scout Groups have to be self-financing.

Members do not have to be practising Christians but all members are expected to follow a faith.

Since the 1940s there have always been more Cubs than Scouts in the UK movement. An even younger section, Beavers, was introduced in 1982.

Scouting has been run in hospitals (still is), orphanages, borstals, factories, at Buckingham Palace and even in prisoner of war camps.

The UK Scout movement reached its numerical highest (including adults and children) in 1988 with 676,988 paid up members.

Wolf Cubs in the 1930s needed (among other items) for their Collectors Badge: 100 postcards in an album, or 200 cigarette pictures in a book.

Scouts in the 1960s were encouraged to wear the special Scout 'Wayfinder' shoes manufactured in East Tilbury. The Scout Association received thousands of pounds for the movement through the sales of these shoes (which had special animal tracks on the sole).

The most popular Scout proficiency badges over the decades have been the Cook, Swimmer, and Camper badges.

Historian Elleke Boehmer comments: *The global reach of the Scout movement has probably been the most extensive of any worldwide. Since its inception Scouting has involved close on 350 million people across the globe and today exists in nearly all of the world's countries, bar 5 or 6.*

The Scouts have made it into the *Guinness Book of Records* on numerous occasions. Two examples include: Scout Graeme Hurry of the 38th Coventry. He was not in a hurry to get indoors: in 1980 he appeared in the *Guinness Book of Records* under 'Camping out'. By 1980 he'd completed 4 years sleeping out, never spending a night indoors.

In 1969 five Scouts from Biggleswade entered the *Guinness Book of Records* for tying 76,504 knots. 50 hours and 30 minutes saw the 9th Bedfordshire Scouts, appearing on Blue Peter, earn £60.00 for charity (though one Scout ended up with a skin allergy after handling the four and a half miles of tarred rope).

As recently as 2006, a Beaver Scout from Surrey was invested outside 10 Downing Street.

Of the twelve Apollo astronauts, eleven were former Boy Scouts. In 1969 Neil Armstrong, a former Eagle Scout, was the first man to set foot on the moon. He left behind scientific equipment for experiments, and a Scout badge.

Scouting's founder was ambidextrous, liked pig-sticking, greeted boys with 'ugly', and slept on his balcony with his toes outside the blankets!

Politics: Sir Harold Wilson, Sir John Major, Tony Benn and Neil Kinnock are all former Scouts.

With over 28 million Scouts, the Scout movement is the world's largest voluntary uniformed youth movement.

Early starters outside the British Empire: Boy Scout organisations were started in Chile and Russia in 1909.

In world-wide Scouting, the movement is growing. In former Communist countries Scouting is enjoying a revival. America and Asia have the highest Scout memberships in the world (in 2006):

> Indonesia ~ 8,103, 835
>
> United States ~ 5, 970, 203
>
> Philippines ~ 1, 872, 525

Text by Steven Harris

The most recent members of the World Scout Organisation are: Albania, Guinea and Malawi.

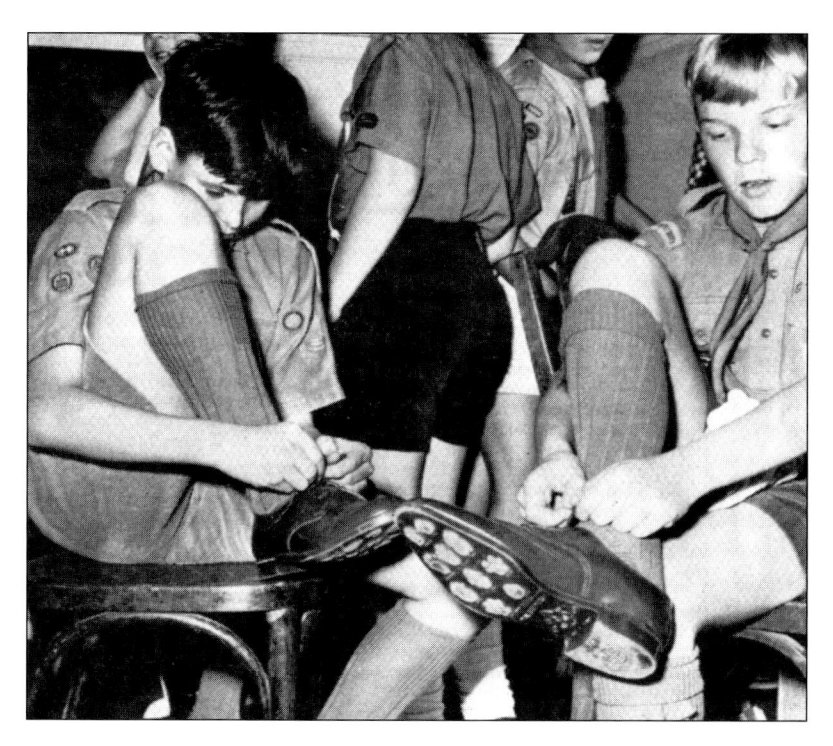

# BROWNSEA ISLAND: DID YOU KNOW?

Without the island of Brownsea, in Poole, Dorset, would it all have happened? Had the Isle of Wight not been such a popular tourist trap even in those days (and a favourite hideaway of Queen Victoria) then perhaps this island would have become known as the Isle of Scout! B.-P. had visited it the year before to inspect some cadets. The idyllic Brownsea Island was where Baden-Powell chose to hold his now famous experimental boys' camp in the summer of 1907. It was reasonably accessible and less likely to attract crowds or the media. Editor of *The Scout* paper Rex Hazlewood would later say: *Once Scouting, one might say, was an island, and soon afterwards, it was a book.*

Fire! Brownsea has had the bad luck of three fires, two being serious. (Erroneous local gossip liked to say that one had been started by local Sea Scouts though Scouts, along with almost everyone else, had not been allowed to visit the island for years.)

The guest rooms in the van Raaltes' castle were named after shrubs and wild flowers. They also kept a rare collection of instruments in the castle. A 'Glasschord' (a keyboard instrument also known as a Pianino) from the collection can be viewed by visitors to Dean Castle, Scotland.

January 1963 saw nearly 100 Scouts, Guides, Scouters and Guiders spend a mammoth icy-cold day (followed by others in later months) in felling trees, draining swamps and clearing undergrowth to make an attractive campsite in preparation for the Scout movement's Diamond Jubilee year in 1967.

Brownsea has had numerous other names and spellings, for example: Brunksey and Branksy.

Brownsea has had some strange characters too. One owner was known as 'Mad Benson'. Around 1710 William Benson bought the island for £300. Although he added much to the island, he suffered a nervous breakdown. He was nicknamed Mad Benson by locals because it was rumoured he practised black magic. In 1735 a servant girl vanished from the island. Local gossip was that she had been the victim of his penchant for necromancy. Fishermen reported hearing blood-curdling screams emanating from the woods on Brownsea!

A successor to Benson, Sir Augustus Foster, also had depressive tendencies and slit his own throat in the castle.

After 1870 the Government wanted to buy Brownsea and establish a naval cadet school on the island.

The population of Brownsea Island in 1881 was: 270. In the 1920s (after the collapse of the island's clay/pottery industry) it was c125. In 2006 there were about 30 residents who lived on Brownsea all year round.

Author Enid Blyton, who used to come and stay in the area, used Brownsea as the setting for one of her stories, called it 'Whispering Island'.

Coincidentally, Brownsea's owner Charles van Raalte was born in 1857: the same year as B.-P. Sadly, just as Scouting was emerging in January 1908, van Raalte suffered an early death and never lived to see the seeds of his own special contribution to B.-P.'s new scheme for boys.

There was/is considerable wildlife on the island, including deer, peacocks, golden pheasants and a rare group of red squirrels (some of these animals made good eating during the war years). Charles van Raalte himself kept a pet monkey.

In 1906 Charles and Florence van Raalte published an island guide book. It contained water colour scenes of Brownsea painted by Florence.

In 1967 two of the original Brownsea Island Scouts were invited to New York by CBS Television to take part in a programme called *'I've Got A Secret'*.

*The Scouter* magazine of 1961 mentioned that: *arrangements have been made for a party of fifty Scouts to visit Brownsea Island on the evening of 7th July, when they will be shown round by the owner. If this visit is a success the owner has promised to allow more.*

*Camping on the island is impossible, since there is only a very limited supply of water within the castle itself and there is, at the moment, no space on which to camp and the fire risk is high.*

Sandbanks, the mainland point from where some of the Brownsea boys set off, is said to be the fourth most expensive place to live in the world. Footballer Jamie Redknapp and celebrities such as Max Bygraves and Bruce Forsyth own properties there (the latter also shares B.-P.'s birthday).

B.-P. had hoped to hold a second Scout camp on Brownsea in 1908, but as he was at that time based in the north of England, a site near Hexham (Humshaugh), Northumbrian Moors, was chosen.

Although the owner of the island, Charles van Raalte, was both supportive and helpful, B.-P. still incurred unexpected expenses which led to the camp being run at a loss. Raalte had offered B.-P. the use of his steam launch, boats, waggons and various staff. It turned out that, being the summer period and a Bank Holiday, some of the staff were not keen to be doing what they probably considered extra chores. B.-P. found himself finding and paying his own baggage handlers, cook and food suppliers.

The Brownsea boys were asked to bring shorts to the camp - a rare thing in 1907 - and to learn three knots.

Poole Harbour is the world's second largest natural harbour, being pipped at the post by Sydney Harbour. Poole Harbour and its neighbouring coastline is peculiar in having a double tide every 12 hours.

Donald was the son of B.-P.'s brother George. Only nine at the time, he went along as B.-P.'s 'adjutant'. He was brave enough to later admit in an interview that he did not wholly enjoy his Brownsea experience. He must have enjoyed his Scouting though! Donald attended the two other famous B.-P. camps: Humshaugh in 1908, and the Beauliea Sea Scout camp, 1909 (John, Rudyard Kipling's son, also attended the 1909 camp). Donald went on to become a distinguished Oxford professor and geologist.

Henry Robson, B.-P.'s camp quartermaster, became Mayor of Bournemouth in 1915 and, later, Deputy Lieutenant of Hampshire. He revisited Brownsea in 1927 with 500 Scouters for the Bournemouth Scouting Conference.

One of the Brownsea Boy Scouts, Arthur Primmer, was a sickly boy. The camp and his later Scouting career must have been good for him: he lived to be over 90! In fact, as Registrar for Poole, even at the age of ninety (in the 1980s) he was still working as a registrar part-time.

Charles van Raalte was elected Mayor of Poole, unusually without being required to first serve as a councillor.

Lord Baden-Powell was granted the Freedom of Poole in 1929 (Olave Baden-Powell also, in 1950).

Although Mrs. Bonham Christie, the van Raaltes' successor (in 1927) and last private owner of the island, became a recluse and never allowed anyone to visit Brownsea, she did permit 500 Scouts to camp there in 1932. This was to celebrate the 25th anniversary of B.-P.'s experimental camp. After, the island once again lived up to its nickname 'The Forbidden Island' (or the 'Mystery Island').

How appropriate that Brownsea should be used for trialling B.-P.'s Boy Scout ideas - a scheme involving observation, rescue and life-saving. In 1906 (a year before the camp) the owner's son, Noel van Raalte, was granted a Diploma from the Royal Humane Society for an act of bravery. Aged fifteen, he'd rescued J. R. Poole from drowning in Poole Harbour. (Aboard the *Arcadian*, Noel accompanied B.-P. on his world tour in 1912.)

Almost half the Scouts at the Brownsea Camp were members of the Boys' Brigade. One of them recalled that when they arrived the tents were already up. Some of the College boys had arrived the day before.

The Brownsea boys had been ferried to Brownsea on the *Hyacinth*, which belonged to the long established local firm of Harvey's Boats. In 1953 it was stolen and later found wrecked off the Isle of Wight. The commemorative plaque from the boat is now displayed in the Museum of the Boy Scouts of Canada.

In 2000, twenty trees were planted at the original campsite used by B.-P., one for each of the boys who attended the first-ever Boy Scout Camp.

By 1852 Brownsea was said to have increased in value, costing its new owner, Colonel Waugh, £1300.

In 1962 the National Trust paid £125,000 to acquire Brownsea Island (the Scout and Guide Associations contributed £20,000). In May 1963 B.-P.'s wife, Lady Olave Baden-Powell (World Chief Guide), planted a Mulberry tree opposite the entrance to the island church, St. Mary the Virgin. This was to celebrate the special camping rights given to the Scout and Guide Associations and to officially declare Brownsea open to the public.

An adult return ferry ticket to the island in 1967 cost 4/-. The price in 2007: £4.50.

In January 1994 Colonel Brian Evans-Lombe, OBE, the last surviving member of the original Brownsea Island Camp, died aged 100.

In 2001 an RAF helicopter made a special delivery of sand and gravel so that volunteers could renovate a pathway leading to the original campsite.

One of John Sweet's many popular *Scouting* magazine cartoons

'He says he got his love of the open-air life from his grandfather who picked it up at a camp of some sort on an island or something many years ago.'

1907 – 2007

The Camp was supposed to be 'hush, hush', but Pearson couldn't resist a report in his *Daily Express* of 1st August 1907!

### BOY SCOUTS IN CAMP. "TREASURE ISLAND" IN BOURNEMOUTH BAY.

#### "EXPRESS" Special Correspondent, Poole, Wednesday Night.

Visitors to Bournemouth know well by sight the little island known as Branksea, lying in the almost landlocked bay at the head of which is this ancient port; but the foot of the ordinary tourist is not often set on this romantic island, which is at present the happy hunting ground of General Baden-Powell and his corps of boy scouts.

The island is the property of Mr. Van Raalte, who has a lovely old castle at the seaward end, looking across to the long line of great sandhills that form the western extremity of Bournemouth.

A few cottages at the little island's harbour, a few more at the northern end, looking across the water to Poole, and a few scattered keepers' lodges constitute the permanent abodes on the island, which is about a mile and a half long and rather less across.

This afternoon I ran down the bay in a motor-boat from Poole to the castle, and then I set out on foot to track the scouts to their lair.

#### "TRACKLESS" FORESTS.

The greater part of the island is covered with forests of pine and beech trees, with thick undergrowth and sand tracks. The woods were so dense and the air was so still, save for the chirping of innumerable birds and the quacking of wild duck on little meres, that I thought for a time that I had discovered "Treasure Island" anew.

At last I saw a kind of "Spyglass Hill," with a few pines on top, and when I had climbed it I saw, down by the shore below, the little-all-alone camp of the scouts. There was one large tent - the mess tent - flanked by two smaller ones. These two are the sleeping places of the General and of Major McLaren, an old fellow soldier who is helping him to train the scouts. As I reached the little camp I spied a tall, thin man, bareheaded, with his jacket and waistcoat off, disappearing further over the hillside. I anticipated what I heard - that it was "B.-P." off on the trail by himself.

There were about a dozen scouts in camp this afternoon, and the rest were due to-night. There will be twenty in all. Those who had arrived were putting up their own tents under the major's directions, and when they had finished the job they fetched trusses of hay, on which, covered with a waterproof, they will sleep.

#### NO DIVISIONS OF RANK.

Some of them are Eton and Harrow lads, some belong to boys' brigades, but all boys are boys when General Baden-Powell has the handling of them, and there are no artificial divisions of rank. The little camp promises to be one of the most delightful memories of these youngsters, for the hero of Mafeking intends teaching them how to follow the trail, how to find a few grains of Indian corn in an acre of heather, and how to hide and discover messages....

## B.-P.'s Last Message to Scouts

My dear Scouts,

If you have ever seen the play 'Peter Pan,' you will remember how the Pirate Chief was always making his dying speech because he was afraid that possibly when the time came for him to die he might not have time to get it off his chest. It is much the same with me; and so, although I am not at this moment dying, I shall be doing so one of these days, and I want to send you a parting word of goodbye.

Remember, it is the last you will ever hear from me - so think it over.

I have had a most happy life, and I want each of you to have as happy a life too.

I believe God put us in this jolly world to be happy and enjoy life. Happiness doesn't come from being rich, nor merely from being successful in your career; nor by self-indulgence. One step towards happiness is to make yourself healthy and strong while you are a boy, so that you can be useful and so can enjoy life when you are men.

Nature Study will show you how full of beautiful and wonderful things God has made the world for you to enjoy. Be contented with what you have got and make the best of it: look on the bright side of things instead of the gloomy one.

But the real way to get happiness is by giving out happiness to other people. Try and leave this world a little bit the better than you found it, and when your turn comes to die you can die happy in feeling that at any rate you have not wasted your time but have done your best.

'Be Prepared' in this way to live happy and to die happy and God help you to do it. Stick to your Scout Promise always - even after you have ceased to be a boy.

Your friend,

*Robert Baden-Powell*

# ~ THE SCOUT LAW AND PROMISE 2007 ~

On my honour I promise that I will do my best
To do my duty to God and the Queen
To help other people
And to keep the Scout Law

1. A Scout is to be trusted.
2. A Scout is loyal.
3. A Scout is friendly and considerate.
4. A Scout belongs to the world-wide family of Scouts.
5. A Scout has courage in all difficulties.
6. A Scout makes good use of time and is careful of possessions and property.
7. A Scout has self-respect and respect for others.

The Scout Motto 1907 - 2007: 'Be Prepared'

### ~ The UK Scout Sections Today ~

Beavers 6 - 8; Cub Scouts 8 - 10$_{1/2}$; Scouts 10$_{1/2}$ - 14; Explorer Scouts 14 - 18; Scout Network 18 - 25

# SOME KEY SCOUTING EVENTS

1857 Robert Stephenson Smyth Baden Powell, Scouting's Founder, born in London, 22nd February.
1900 **MAY** Baden-Powell finds fame during the Boer War as one of the great defenders of Mafeking.
1907 **AUG** Brownsea Island Camp.
1908 **JAN** *Scouting for Boys* published in parts.
**APR** *The Scout* paper launched.
**AUG** Humshaugh Camp with B.-P.
1909 **AUG** Sea Scout Camp, Hamble, Southampton.
**SEP** First National Rally, at the Crystal Palace.
1910 Girl Guides Founded.
1911 Windsor Rally/review by the King.
1912 **JAN** Royal Charter for the Boy Scouts.
**OCT** Marriage of B.-P. to Olave Soames.

Text by Steven Harris

| | | |
|---|---|---|
| **1914** | **AUG** | Start of 1st World War, Scouts utilised. |
| **1916** | | Wolf Cubs officially launched. |
| **1917** | | Rover Scout Scheme started. |
| **1919** | **JUL** | Gilwell Park officially opened. |
| | **SEP** | First Wood Badge course held. |
| **1920** | **JUL** | First World Jamboree held at London's Olympia, B.-P. declared Chief Scout of the World. |
| **1929** | **JUL** | Arrowe Park 'Coming of Age' Jamboree. |
| **1932** | **OCT** | First of Ralph Reader's Gang Shows. |
| **1939** | | First Soap Box derby held at Brooklands. |
| **1939** | **SEP** | Start of the 2nd World War, Scouts again help by: guarding reservoirs, the coast, evacuation.... |
| **1941** | **JAN** | B.-P., Scouting's Founder, dies in Kenya. Air Scout branch begins. |
| **1946** | | Senior Scouts started. |
| **1949** | | Bob-a-Job fundraising scheme started. |
| **1952** | | Berets permitted as alternative to big hat. |
| **1957** | | 9th World Jamboree held at Sutton Coldfield. |
| **1961** | **JUL** | Baden-Powell House and hostel opened by H M The Queen. |
| **1961** | | Long uniform trousers permitted as alternative to shorts for older Scouts and leaders. |
| **1962** | | The National Trust purchased Brownsea Island. |
| **1963** | **MAY** | Brownsea Island opened to public. |
| **1966** | **JUN** | The Chief Scout's *Advance Party Report* published: major changes to uniform and programme. |
| **1967** | | Diamond Jubilee of Scouting. |
| **1971** | | New purple World Membership badge introduced. |
| **1977** | **JUN** | Lady Olave Baden-Powell, World Chief Guide, dies. |
| **1982** | | New younger section, 'Beavers', introduced. |
| **1990** | | Girls could be permitted into the younger Scout sections if Scout Groups wished. |
| **1994** | **JAN** | Colonel Brian Evans-Lombe OBE, the only surviving member of the original Brownsea Island Camp, died aged 100. |
| **2000** | **MAY** | Millennium Camps held throughout the UK. |
| **2002** | | Launch of new uniforms, sections and training programmes. |
| **2004** | **APR** | Betty Clay, CBE, the B.-P.'s last surviving daughter, dies. |
| | **SEP** | Former *Blue Peter* presenter, Peter Duncan, invested as the new (ninth) Chief Scout. |
| **2007** | | World Centenary Jamboree at Hylands Park, Chelmsford, Essex, England. |

# BIBLIOGRAPHY

*The First Ten Years,* Percy Everett, 1948

*Legalised Mischief,* The History of the Scout Movement From a Grassroots Perspective, Steven Harris, 2006

*Baden-Powell: The Two Lives of a Hero,* William Hillcourt with Olave Baden-Powell, 1964

*Baden-Powell,* Tim Jeal, 1989

*Don Potter: An Inspiring Century,* Vivienne Light, 2002

*Why Brownsea?,* Brian Woolgar and Sheila La Riviere, 2003

# ACKNOWLEDGEMENTS

Sincere thanks go to John Roberts for proof-reading the typescript; and also grateful thanks to the following: Poole Historical Trust, Keith Russell, the National Trust, Ayr Future Museum, John F Rickard, Mary Potter, Alan Shrimpton and Bryanston Art School, The Story of Scouting Museum, the British Library, the Borough of Poole Local History Centre, 1st Par Scout Group and Sally Tregaskes, The Scout Association.

For a detailed history of the Scout movement, see the unique series *Legalised Mischief.* Written by the author, the volumes contain photographs, interviews and a decade by decade account of the movement's development, particularly at a grassroots level. Further details can be found at: www.lewarnepublishing.co.uk